WHEN *Angels* SPEAK

Messages from the Keepers of The Lion's Gate

*To Anne —
who looks like
an angel.
Donna Wolfe
June 1998*

WHEN *Angels* SPEAK

Messages from the Keepers of The Lion's Gate

Nadira Duran & Donna Wolfe

I AM Publishing
Salem, Oregon

Copyright © 1997 Donna Gatti
Published by I AM Publishing
3760 Augusta National Drive, South
Salem, Oregon 97302

ISBN 0-9658290-0-6

All rights reserved. No part of this book may be reproduced without permission from the publisher, except by a reviewer who may quote brief passages in a review; nor may any part of this book be reproduced, stored in a retrieval system, or copied by mechanical photocopying, recording, or other means without permission of the publisher.

The illustration on page 13, titled *The Lion's Gate*, is by Gary Wolfe. It is contributed by Patty Wolfe, Phoenix, Arizona.

Cover Design: *Design Studio Selby*

5 4 3 2 1

Cataloging in Publication Data

Duran, Nadira.
    When angels speak : messages from the keepers of the Lion's gate / Nadira Duran, Donna Wolfe. -- 1st ed.
    p. cm.

1. Spirit writings. 2. Angels--Miscellanea. I. Wolfe, Donna J.

BF1290.D87 1997   133.9'3
                                         QBI97-40521

Printed in the United States of America

CONTENTS

A Divine Invitation • 1

THE KEEPERS OF THE LION'S GATE

King Solomon • 15

Archangel Raphael • 23

Chadeau, Protector of the Children • 31

Archangel Gabriel • 43

Sundar Singh, Ascended Master Teacher • 55

Archangel Uriel • 61

Carmen, Protector of the Abused • 73

Archangel Michael • 81

Isaac, Son of Sarah and Abraham • 89

Mary, Mother of Jesus • 97

Prophet Muhammad • 105

Vyada, Universal Master Teacher • 115

Queen Esther • 123

Reflections • 131

The Authors • 135

ACKNOWLEDGMENTS

We are deeply grateful to the angels on earth who generously gave so much of themselves—their time, their brilliance, and especially their love—to assist the heavenly angels in the creation of this book. Our most heartfelt thanks goes to: Stephanie and Scott McIntyre, David Stakem, Patricia M. and Clarence E. Wolfe, Patricia A. Wolfe, David McCallum, John Tillman and Barrett Tillman, the John W. Dixon Family, and all the other members of the Brotherhood of White Light.

This little book is lovingly dedicated
to the Creator of heaven and earth.

A DIVINE INVITATION

Donna

In January of 1992 I made an appointment with Nadira Duran to meet my guardian angel. Direct contact with my personal angel seemed too good to be true, but I was willing to take the chance. I had gone to Nadira for counseling eight years earlier, two years before she received the gift of channeling, and her advice was incredibly accurate. I trusted her and thought if it was possible to communicate with angels, Nadira would know how to do it.

The world of the mysterious and the inexplicable intrigued me even as a child, but especially so after a near-death experience at the age of twenty-five. During a minor surgical operation "something went wrong" and I lost a great deal of blood, according to the doctor who reported the situation to my family. I—my personality and spirit—floated up and away from my body and I could hear a nurse say, "We're losing her."

I felt serenely calm and unworried. A warm and comforting

field of light surrounded me, and I noticed that two cherubs were at my side. We slowly drifted to the corner of the ceiling and observed the doctors and nurses below.

The light intensified and I had the distinct feeling that I was expected to make a decision. My escorts patiently waited as I looked down at the body on the operating bed and assessed its usefulness. In a detached manner, I judged the problem to be "not serious enough" and whoosh, I reentered my body through the navel, then watched as the angels flew through the wall and disappeared. I still can recall the physical pain of reentry and the unsettling feeling that I had to wait a while longer before I could go "home."

The feeling of homesickness initiated an intense curiosity. Where is *home*? What happened to me? Why do I feel so sad? A voice inside me said, "Try to remember. It will come to you. Just relax." But I couldn't. I knew there was more to this puzzle than I could perceive through my five senses and I could not rest until I had some answers.

I began my quest into the supernatural with a promise to myself—I pledged to be open-minded but skeptical. I reasoned that a closed mind could learn little or nothing about esoteric matters so I would entertain every idea, if only for a moment. A healthy amount of skepticism would allow me to filter out truth from nonsense. I couldn't hope for tangible proof. I had to rely on my personal experiences and reports from others.

More than twenty years have passed since my near-death experience. I have studied many different religions, read countless books, listened to numerous tapes by popular "gurus" and visited anyone who could possibly offer a crumb to satisfy my spiritual hunger, including doctors of both Eastern and Western medicine, psychologists, channelers, hypnotists, astrologers, psychics, tarot card readers, and various other practitioners. My wandering ended when I established a connection with the angels.

Nadira introduced me to my guardian angel Dalia (pronounced Da-LEE-ah) who told me that my name in the spiritual realm is Lucia, which means "one who carries light," and that I had come back to earth to overcome negativity and "climb to higher elevations on the ethereal plane." She said that before I was born I had chosen my family, my friends, and the "negatives and positives" of my life. And I had chosen Dalia herself to be "not an advisor but a reminder" of my spiritual essence.

Dalia talked about painful situations in my life that had caused "many tears to fall upon your pathway." It was comforting to have my guardian angel acknowledge the sadness I had endured. She told me about my future and how it would be very different from my past, and warned me not to follow "those who are lost in darkness." Then she gave me a gift from the spiritual realm. "It is called *honor*. Allow your heart to open and accept the gift of honor, an honoring of your inner being and who you are on this day and in this lifetime."

For seven minutes Dalia talked about my spiritual being and my past lifetimes. When she left I was overwhelmed with emotion and began to cry from joy, I felt peaceful and happy. Now I knew where *home* was—it was in the spiritual world with Dalia, but I couldn't return until I finished my education on earth.

For over three years Dalia and other angels diligently answered my unspoken questions, using Nadira as a transmitter. Many different angels gave me information, depending on the lessons I needed to learn for spiritual growth. They began slowly, teaching me a little at a time. "We feed you milk as you are but a babe," Angel Abraham said. Eventually they asked me to share with the world the knowledge they had so lovingly given me. Who could refuse an angel?

Earth School

Why was I born? What is my purpose? Do I have a destiny? Some of us entertain these questions while sitting under a tree on a hot summer day, others while celebrating a birth in the family. But almost all of us contemplate the meaning of life when faced with a crisis. Our survival instincts kick in and we become more physically and mentally aware. Daily concerns fall away and we look for answers to the big questions.

When we are desperately in need of help we are silently

surrounded by angels. Many humans avoid people in trouble, but neediness is an attractive quality to angels. When we call on angels—out of despair or simply in a small prayer—we give them an opportunity to serve. Through service angels can increase the power of their light.

People are like angels in that we are also eternal light beings, but we are encased in limited, temporary bodies for the purpose of attending earth school. One day we will all graduate, but first we must pass the tests put before us. God wants us to learn, to grow, and to evolve. He has been waiting patiently for us, but now it is time for us to advance.

We all remember going to school. The primary years were pleasurable, but we envied the high school kids. They were cool and had more fun. We couldn't wait to grow up and be teenagers. Earth school is much the same. The farther along we progress spiritually, the more alive we feel. Awareness, wisdom, and knowledge replace self-centeredness, fear, and jealousy. Spiritual maturity frees us from childish emotions.

Archangel Michael

Archangel Michael is the master teacher for this book and we learned to follow his lead through trial and error. When we wrote something he didn't like, the computer would break down or he would "suffer" us until we made the appropriate changes and the feeling of approval would flow through our veins. Once Michael appeared before Nadira with two chapters of the manuscript "X'd" out. Archangels can be very demanding.

Michael showed Nadira the finished book a year before its completion. He changed our title from *The Book of Spirits* to *When Angels Speak*. Although I knew it was hopeless to argue with Michael, I complained that his title was inaccurate because the messengers who channeled through Nadira were not angels. Muhammad was not an angel, he was a prophet. King Solomon and Queen Esther were biblical characters and technically not angels.

Michael did not acknowledge my objections, and his silence spoke loudly to me. He wanted me to figure out this problem on my own, without an easy answer from him. I started my search with the dictionary and found that *angel* means messenger of God. Then I looked in various books about angels, but there were no statements supporting Michael. Finally I turned to my personal channelings, reread them, and found that Dalia had mentioned that some beings were always angels and others acquired the title by performing spiritual works.

Muhammad, Solomon, and Esther had developed angelic qualities while living on earth. Mary, Mother of Jesus, is crowned Queen of the Angels. Can all of us become angels when we graduate from earth school?

Nadira

Nadira's mother Jewell loved to talk about her only daughter. She said Nadira's body "glowed" for eleven days after her birth and people called her "the baby with magic skin." She bragged that at the age of three Nadira began uttering prophecy from the pulpit in their church. During the last few years of her life, Jewell's full-time nurse was Nadira. The doctors often remarked on how her healing powers had prolonged Jewell's life.

After obeying a call from Archangel Michael to go to Arizona and perform spiritual work, Nadira was given the gift of channeling. Angels call her a channel for Spirit* and she can see angels in her mind's eye and hear them speak. She responds to their voices like a United Nations interpreter—when angels talk to her she simply repeats each word out loud. Nadira says she is only an instrument for the angels, a human messenger.

Nadira was told by Archangel Michael that her destiny was to rewrite fourteen books that had been lost in the final days of the Mayan civilization. Her "scribe" would come to her, he promised. Dalia informed me I had the job and, on May 6, 1995, Nadira translated and I transcribed the first of eighteen messages contained in this book.

---

* *Spirit* includes angels, all spiritual beings, the spiritual realm, and God.

The angelic authors of this volume call themselves the Keepers of The Lion's Gate. They are: Archangels Michael, Gabriel, Raphael, and Uriel; Mary, Mother of Jesus; King Solomon; Queen Esther; Isaac, Son of Abraham and Sarah; Chadeau and Carmen, Protectors; Sundar Singh and Vyada, Teachers; and Prophet Muhammad.

I sat with Nadira and tape-recorded most but not all of the translations. Four messages were sent when I wasn't available. Solomon, Michael, and Vyada spoke to Nadira while she was alone and she tape-recorded their transmissions. Nadira wrote Carmen's message in long hand because she was ill with a throat infection and could not speak clearly. All messages were delivered over a span of eighty-three days.*

Angelic Instructions

Dalia and many other angels contributed to this book by providing us with information about content and publishing. They said they were all *at one* in their counseling. Dalia asked me to describe Nadira's "nature" and my "journey" with her, and to "write in simplicity and from the heart." Also, "Every word you write must be the truth."

---

* The messages had to be delivered on specific days designated by the Creator. Spirit could not transmit messages before or after the allotted time frame.

The angels named Faith, Hope, and Charity endowed me with the qualities they represent. I was given Faith to believe in what I cannot see or hear, Hope for the future, and blessings and love from Charity. They share their gifts freely—all anyone has to do is ask.

Angel Zarus said, "On these pages is the Word of Spirit and there is nothing more powerful. These books were written by you before. We will come to you in your dream state to activate your memories. Deliver these messages to the world as they have been spoken and change them in as small a way as possible." With this command some explanations are required.

Angelic language is archaic and Nadira and I were unfamiliar with many of the obsolete words and expressions. Nadira struggled with pronunciation and I with spelling, but the usage was appropriate and the meanings easily understood. Angels generally use masculine gender terms, but this is only another form of archaic speech. Mankind includes men and women, human beings have both masculine and feminine energies. Angels never discriminate against anyone on the basis of sex, race, religion, national origin, politics, behavior, or any other orientation. They love all of us individually and as children of the Creator, and they say we cannot imagine the magnitude and depth of their love.

You may want to reread some passages for hidden implications, which is exactly what the angels want you to do. Like all treasures, the best gems are often overlooked at first. The angels ask you to read this book with your heart and soul, and if a word or phrase "rings the bell of clarity" you will know it was meant for you.

A cosmic plan has been formulated to bring people and angels closer together. One day the ethereal and earthly realms will merge and we will all live in peace. You have taken your first step into this ideal future by picking up this book and reading these sentences, but you are not alone. Angels are ready and willing to guide you on your path. If this assistance is not divine intervention, then it is certainly divine opportunity.

When Angels Speak

Angels speak only the truth. Unlike human beings they do not have free will. They aren't subjected to the moral predicaments of mortals such as, "Should I take the easy way out and lie, or should I tell the truth and face the consequences?" Quite often we say we can't go to dinner, we can't go to work, or we can't help you, when what we really mean is *we don't want to do it*. The truth doesn't sound very nice and we're afraid we won't be liked if we are totally honest. Angels are not permitted to utter the smallest lie. They must tread the straight and narrow pathway of truth.

Angels speak words of love. They are always tender and

kind, they never nag or complain. While I was writing this book the angels frequently pointed out my mistakes and shortcomings, but they did so to help me. Not once did they hurt my feelings by being nasty or sarcastic, nor did they try to shame me. Through their gentleness I learned and I changed.

We have free will and angels must respect the laws inherent to freedom. They cannot come to us unless we invite them, and even then they need a passageway between heaven and earth. Archangel Michael came to Nadira in 1988 and announced he had begun making preparations for construction of a light corridor, a *spiritual superhighway*, for angelic travel. He said the angels were ready and waiting for his command, and his next task was to collect love energy from humanity, as love is the key to the heavenly gate.

On August 8, 1992, two hours before midnight, the constellation Leo was in perfect alignment for the conception of a light corridor. Michael and his band of angels gathered the necessary quota of human love and, in a secluded area in the Northwest not far from the Pacific Ocean, they dynamited an opening between heaven and earth. The explosion sparked an electrical light-show.

A blast of pure white light erupted from the ground, bolts of lightning streaked through the sky, and huge balls of fire burst in the air. Lights flashed in the darkness every thirteen seconds until shortly after midnight, unseen by the sleeping masses and shown only to the aware.* Then a clash of thunder heralded the birth of The Lion's Gate. The spiritual superhighway was established and multitudes of celestial beings entered the earth.

---

* Spirit protected the opening of The Lion's Gate from view by all but a few. Nadira and two other people in the vicinity witnessed its creation.

The Keepers of The Lion's Gate

The Lion's Gate

The Song of Songs in the Old Testament was written by Solomon, the poet of the Bible. The Song is romantic and endearing, like its author. When Nadira met Solomon he elegantly bowed and offered her a pure, white, *ethereal* rose, more beautiful than the earthly variety, according to our channel. Although Solomon was the last messenger to speak he instructed us to place his message first. He smiled when he gave this order, as if he enjoyed the paradox of giving us the introductory speech to signal the end of the messages.

Proverbs, Ecclesiastes, and Wisdom are also credited to Solomon. He was a sage, divinely endowed with intelligence, wisdom, and an understanding heart. Nadira said the essence of Solomon's powerful attributes charged the air while he spoke.

Angels are very humble and Solomon is no exception. He is modest but self-assured. To dignify his message he said "for I am Solomon." Many angels use this expression to validate their announcements; they accept their authority without pride or shame.

To channel for Spirit Nadira has to go through a purification process. First she clears her mind of earthly concerns and concentrates on Spirit. Next she closes her eyes and imagines herself entering a tunnel. Then light beings appear to escort her to the angel in waiting.

To meet with Solomon Nadira had to pass through the Purple Flame. This is a test of courage because the flame looks like real fire. Intellectually she knew that her ethereal body could not burn, but fear is a natural, human reaction to fire. As she entered the flame, the deep purple colors changed to various shades of lavender. Then a rectangular platform of emerald green lights known as Cosmic Consciousness, which is alive with energy and life, descended to the floor. Nadira stepped on and it carried her to King Solomon's domain.

King Solomon Speaks

I bid you welcome. I am filled with overwhelming joy because you have entered my doorway. I am Solomon and my song comes forth from the light corridor known as The Lion's Gate—a passageway aligning with the constellation Leo but originating on the heavenly levels.

It is through this gate that we may enter the earth's realm and our workers can physically manifest themselves to you, if necessary. These angels are here to help individuals who are specifically chosen according to their spiritual works. They also give healing energy to the earth from outward-inward and from inward-outward. It is important for you to know that there are many angels who walk and talk amongst you.

Azi Azon, the Ancient,* has delivered many messages from those who have preceded me. Is it not an oddity that my song is sung last but will be first to be heard? All things are such a mystery!

---

* Nadira's name in the spiritual realm.

We of the spiritual realm are most grateful to you, the Ancient, for delivering our messages. Bless your hearts, each one of you, who chooses by your own free will to help us reach other kindred spirits searching for their own ring of truth. The truth will resound harmoniously inside their breasts, for the Word and its significance to the great I AM will be the beginning of peace for the soul and the redeemer of spiritual freedom.

You, the helpers of this Ancient, will be reunited upon the earth once again for your communion. All of you are acknowledged and highly praised, for you are members of the Brotherhood of White Light and we from The Lion's Gate glorify you. We pray you will be rewarded in heaven and on earth. And surely it is so.

It is now necessary for you to know about The Lion's Gate which is an energy corridor, a portal, that brings forth angels with messages from the Akashic Records.* This gate was opened again on August 8, 1992, and it was given enough light energy for a limited number of years. It will remain open only if you make the changes we ask for in this book. These changes, which begin in your heart and radiate outward, will help us continue to work on earth. Thus, a new era will begin again for mankind.

---

* The Akashic Records contain knowledge of all events, both large and small, that have occurred on earth since its creation. Also, all the thoughts, feelings, and actions of every human being are recorded in his or her Book of Life. These records are kept in a library called the Hall of Knowledge.

I ask forgiveness if I have confused you by saying the gate was opened again, but surely you must know that what has been will be again and what will be has already been. Read the words, for I am Solomon and I have spoken correctly to you. When you read these pages pray for understanding and patience, for they are the foundation of wisdom.

This is what we are: We are the Keepers of The Lion's Gate, we are this book, and only you can turn the pages. It matters not what religion you are, what is your race, your education, or your wealth. What does matter is your works upon this earth.

This is why we are here: We are here to give you knowledge. When you first look upon our pages we will show you wisdom, but as you study our words the veils worn by wisdom will fall away and the pure I AM will be waiting for your discovery.

So I come forth on this day to ask that you take heed to our words. This is our song for this lovely world and all the children upon it. Listen carefully, and when you are ready we bid you to sing with us. I am Solomon.

Selah.

Archangel Raphael

King Solomon delivered the introduction, but Raphael's message came first. Nadira and I had been told by many angels that the time was right to begin channeling for this book, but we were very nervous about the project. Nadira estimated she had conducted over two thousand channelings, but all of them had been personal readings meant for the spiritual development and enlightenment of an individual—this message was for the world. Why I was the designated "scribe" was a mystery to me and I was afraid I would disappoint the angels.

Dalia knew of our anxiety and asked us not to worry. She said, "Do not fail in your faith or in your belief or in your hope, for if you do we cannot assist you. We breathe the being of these elements and without them our existence fades." All that we needed would be given to us, she promised, and the angels named Wisdom, Clarity, and Reassurance were ready and waiting for our summons. There are more angels than grains of sand on a beach and they are on standby at all times for a call from humanity.

We gathered up our courage and prepared to channel. Instead of sitting to Nadira's right as I would for a personal reading, I sat directly across from her. She had to focus on conveying a universal message and we didn't want my energy to distract her. When we were settled we looked at each other, bowed our heads in prayer, and waited to receive.

Within a few minutes Raphael appeared to Nadira and began his speech. He had given personal messages to us before so we immediately relaxed. We knew this channeling session would be successful and powerful because of Raphael's prominence in the spiritual world. It is very difficult for high angels like Raphael to lower their vibration rate to enter the earth's realm, so they appear only for important matters.

Raphael manifested himself as a glorious butterfly made of rose-colored lights with a vertical yellow light nestled inside his wings. After he finished his speech he changed his colors to a rainbow of greens, purples, and blues and floated out of sight.

Archangel Raphael Speaks

Words are only words. The people were given the power of the Word and, through their individual interpretations, they have created mighty nations.

I am Raphael and I come forth to enfold you in my wings of love. Many of you have become hardened in this world of materiality, and it is not for the material that you are here. You are here for your love of the universe and its elements—the earth, the water, the air, the fire—and the energy created from these blessings. I say that all things wonderful and good come from our blessed Creator.

I have come from far beyond the dimensions of this universe, even though I was once in physical form like you. I have seen through man's eyes, as it was deemed necessary for me to do so. I suffered greatly at the hands of others, but I gained compassion and understanding.

I wish to speak about man's soul. Each one of you comes from a pure, spiritual, soul-body. When you are born into the physical world you are given *fire* and *life* inside your soul, which create an electrical force. Electricity is part of the universe and all of the earth's domain. Along with electricity you are given another significant energy called *rhythm*, the music of your soul.

Many people have given up their God-gifted rhythm because their earthly desires have not been fulfilled. You are not here to satisfy your fleeting desires. You are here to sing your song, to live in harmony, and to overcome negative energies accumulated in prior lifetimes. It has caused us grave concern to see you so easily give up your souls for gold or vanity or lust—these things are trifles in the universe. You must raise your standards.

Everyone on earth must undergo their trials and tribulations. Some of you learn from your troubles, accept them as part of life, and go on to become great in the eyes of Spirit. Some of you become lost in darkness and cannot see the spiritual pathway that is lit just for you. I am Raphael and I am here to guide you. I am here to offer hope for those of you who have given up. I am here for your salvation.

It is a heartbreaking certainty that those who choose to behave like wild beasts without a mind or a conscience will reverse their *wheel of life** and darken their souls. In times past, the reversal of the wheel dropped men to their knees and destroyed

---

* Everything and everyone in the universe are constantly moving. If we aren't progressing we are regressing, and our wheel of life goes either forward or backward.

civilizations. We are here from the spiritual domains to stop this from happening, but we are limited by the free will of mankind. You must choose to change your lives. You must choose to rise above the darkness of evil and the loneliness and seclusion of one who is not walking the pathway of the Creator.

The Lion's Gate and The Angel's Gate* have brought forth many light beings who give wisdom and knowledge to those they contact. They are the comforters and at times they are also the victims.

There will come upon the earth a great transformation. You will see a division between good and evil. We come forth to speak the Word to those who are seeking and these seekers can light the way for others. No one in darkness is truly happy. Their reflection tells them so.

---

* The Angel's Gate light corridor was opened in 1986 in Arizona and Nadira was there for its creation.

CHADEAU

PROTECTOR OF THE CHILDREN

No matter how old you are, you are a child in the eyes of Spirit and Chadeau (pronounced Cha-DAY-oo) is your protector. Chadeau is the general of the Angelic Army and he has the power to send his soldiers to our rescue at the first sign of conflict. Many of Chadeau's workers have caught children falling out of trees, escorted the frightened through dark alleys, and hugged the lonely while they slept, but they are not permitted to intervene in destiny.

Sometimes our worst enemy is within—that nasty, annoying voice that tells us we aren't good enough, we're stupid, or we don't deserve. When we are excessively critical of ourselves we develop self-hatred, which can lead to various kinds of destructive behavior—towards others or ourselves. It is a principle of the universe that you can't cause harm to another person without hurting yourself, and a cycle of abuse is established largely because of a lack of self-love.

Queen Esther, in one of her directives for this book, said, "We in the spiritual realm gaze down upon you in wonderment.

Do you have any idea how precious you are? You have such grace and beauty and innocence—do you not know of your value? You are the children of the Creator and your inheritance is heaven." Angels shower us with raindrops of love and, if such magnificent beings love us, we must be very special.

    Angels use colors to intensify the meaning of their words. A display of a certain shade of green facilitates health and well-being, but a different tone is used to indicate spiritual prosperity and another for material wealth. Since everything is interrelated in the sight of Spirit, most angels arrive in an array of multicolored lights. For Chadeau's three messages he chose yellow for knowledge, green for healing, and red for love.

Chadeau Speaks

First Message

Greetings. It is I, Chadeau, and I come forth for your enlightenment.

I wish to speak of *star children*, the new souls coming through the light corridor. These children will be different from others because Akashic knowledge has been planted inside their souls. They will possess angelic virtues, they will be loving and good. They will detest wrongdoing and the malicious ways of evil, they will denounce the darkness and stamp it out. Some are here now and many more are coming.

Many people have become addicted to drugs and alcohol, and these chemicals have mutated and damaged their genes and chromosomes. Children born to these people will be genetically addicted and, in each succeeding generation, the chromosomes will mutate even more. This is an abomination to the Creator of the universe who made all things perfect and new.

Star children are coming forth to counterbalance this degeneration because, if something is not done soon, the earth will surely perish—like Sodom and Gomorrah. The genetic and soulular* makeup of humanity will continue to deteriorate until the negative energies completely overcome the positive. You will see a more violent, vicious, and morally decadent race than you have ever seen before. You are viewing some of this now, but it will become much worse in the future.

I am the Protector of the Children and I come forth to defend them. I have seen much sadness and pain inflicted on children by their addicted parents. Some of these children are now in their twenties and others are in their first year of life. Their parents, family, and friends have treated these children like possessions. They have not glorified them for their abilities. They have not declared them perfect, created in God's love. We in the spiritual realm cry for the children who are punished merely for being born.

To those of you who cast your net of love to a sea of people while throwing your own children aside—I say it is an abomination! The same love and friendship you devote to others can be used to cultivate the seeds you have planted on this earth. You are here to guide your children. Your guidance is so important, especially in the beginning. Children's early years form the foundation for all their days on earth.

---

* *Soulular* is a word coined by Spirit and means *pertaining to the soul.*

The War of the Drug Lord will come to an end with a flickering of the Creator's hand. Addictions have swept across this country, creating the decay of moral fiber and the decadence of society. Through the loss of morality, many people have slipped into random sexual activities that have generated diseases that will annihilate this planet.

You must realize your purpose in being on this planet—not the devil's purpose but the Creator's. It is not your desires, your lusts, or your greed that you should consider. You must accept your responsibility to your own children, lest you be struck with barrenness and *humanity will cease to exist*. If you do not guard and protect the children, there will not be a future.

I do not speak these words to cause fear in your hearts, but to awaken the seed of love God planted inside your souls. I come forth to nurture that seed, to cultivate it, and to allow love to grow and produce the Garden of Eden earth was intended to be.

Chadeau Speaks

Second Message

Yea, it is I, Chadeau. I am here to glorify the Creator and you, His children. My message is for the youth on this planet, but my words will ring true to all of you.

Within each of you beats the heart and soul of Mother Earth. You have felt her pain and sorrow as she was girdled with contamination and the stresses of greed and evil, and you have felt her vibrations as she cried out for compassion and love. Her suffering has affected all of you, but you are not responsible for her distress. It was caused by those who came before you, many ages ago. Your anger is understandable, and I have come to comfort you.

If only I could enfold you in my wings and cleanse you from all suffering and sorrow, I say I surely would, but it is not within my empowerment. You are here to learn. Earth is a school that prepares you to confront and overcome evil. First you must recognize it, and on every turn of your head you will be able to do so. Realize that evil is patient. It waits for the opportune time to strike, such as when you feel your life has no meaning.

When you feel all is lost and you have been emotionally abandoned by family and friends, do not be discouraged. When people say you look odd or dress strangely, do not be dismayed. When they point their fingers and say you cannot achieve, do not be disheartened. Rise up and show your accusers love and happiness. Know that you are special to all of us in the spiritual world, and especially to the Creator.

You are the Master's gardeners. Sow seeds of faith, hope, and charity, and you will harvest an abundance of love. Begin by planting these seeds within your family and forgive your parents—they are but children who have grown older. They are suffering from their own heartaches and the worries of daily living. One day you will understand.

I say that I am with you. I was with you in the beginning and I will be with you always. Not one cry goes out in the darkness that I do not hear. Not one tear falls from your eyes that is not felt by my heart. I embrace you with love.

Our smiles shine down blessings of love upon you. Each one of you is a flower in the Master's bouquet. Create your love, radiate your love, share it freely. Let the earth blossom once more.

Selah.

Chadeau Speaks

Third Message

Yea, greetings my beloved ones. It is I, Chadeau, and I come forth to hold you in my wings and radiate love upon you from our Father and all the angels in heaven.

I am the Protector of the Children and today I come forth for the elderly—those whose physical bodies have aged and, quite often, their emotional bodies too. But their souls are timeless—they stay young forever.

In ancient times the elderly were called *storytellers* and were held in high regard by the younger generations. In today's culture the voices of the elders are not heard, but they too have their stories. They too nursed at their mothers' breasts, as all of you have. They too were young and strong and vigorous. I am here to remind you that time is a robber of one's desires and strengths. Time will take away your youth. Time will take away your patience. Time will take away your hopes and dreams.

As you look upon the elders you will see this is true.

As people age they become more fragile and in need of emotional support. If they are not loved and respected, they lose their sense of identity. The elders so desire to give and receive love, but most often they are disregarded and laughed at as if they were mental incompetents. Indeed, many of the young in this society consider them little more than burdens.

Everyone needs to be loved, for love is essential in your passing to our world. If you feel lonely and unloved, your transformation into the afterlife will be difficult. You will have to find the strength to overcome loneliness, for loneliness is undying.

I unfold my wings to spread words of understanding—just simple understanding—of everyone's need to be loved, understood, and respected. And the greatest need is love.

To those who are old, thinking about the past always causes pain and sorrow. They lived long and made many mistakes. They sinned, they were greedy, and they were selfish. All this is part of the learning process—you learn from your mistakes. But as the elders sit and reflect on days gone by, they feel such remorse.

I say unto you: Do not reflect! You have learned and learned well. Accept those who love you and accept yourself. When it comes time to go home to God, go with pride and dignity. You are tired from your physical, emotional, and mental ailments, but the tiredness will cease as you release your guilt.

Come into my wings and let me caress you with love. I will

carry you forward to a new day, a new life.

Consider the flowers. As a rosebud blooms then withers and dies, in the following spring a new rose appears. It does not come back as a daffodil, it comes as a rose. So also will you rejuvenate and come again to bloom once more.

Archangel Gabriel

"Gabriel, come blow your horn." This was our request and Gabriel acquiesced. We were extremely excited when Gabriel spoke to us. Nadira and I scheduled book channelings in advance, but we never knew which angel, if any, would choose to appear. When Gabriel declared his presence we felt very honored. And as he spoke he filled the room with love.

No other angel has made as many important announcements as Gabriel, but he is not one to linger and chat. Some angels enjoy speaking and repeat themselves to add emphasis to their words, but not Gabriel. He arrives suddenly, comes quickly to the point, then moves on to his next task.

Arrangements for the birth of Jesus were made by Gabriel. He was sent by God to tell Mary she was to bear a son and, when Mary protested that she could not possibly have a child because she was a virgin, Gabriel answered, "Nothing is impossible to God." Gabriel spoke to Joseph and assured him of Mary's virtue, and later he proclaimed Jesus' birth to the shepherds as they stood watch in the fields.

Gabriel dictated the text of the Koran to Muhammad, even though the prophet was illiterate. The inability to read and write is a small problem to miracle workers. And formal writing experience must not be a prerequisite for "scribes" or I would not have this job. Writing a book seemed like an impossibility to me before the angels told me to do it. "Have faith," they said.

As cited in the Bible, Daniel received the Seventy Weeks Prophecy from Gabriel who began by saying, "Daniel, I have come to give you understanding." In two of the following lessons Gabriel endeavors to help us understand the process of healing. He demonstrated his abilities by curing Nadira's sore throat. While Nadira was on the ethereal plane, Gabriel placed a rose-colored scarf inside her throat. Nadira choked, but the procedure opened her throat passage and eliminated the pain. He used the color rose, which represents love, because "love is the healer."

In his third message Gabriel addresses the leaders of the world. Even the high-and-mighty have to answer to a greater power. In the nicest way possible, angels are demanding peace. They love our planet and want to save it.

To meet with Gabriel Nadira followed tiny light beings on an automated walkway that transported her to a designated meeting place. Gabriel arrived on the emerald green rectangular platform called Cosmic Consciousness, which changed in color to rose as it descended to Nadira's level. Gabriel immediately began to speak.

Archangel Gabriel Speaks

First Message

I bid you glad tidings. I am Gabriel and I have been selected to speak to you. I come forth to convey knowledge of the healing rays of light Archangel Michael shines upon the earth. Every ray of Michael comes forth in love and righteousness. Thus, Michael comes forth to break the darkness, to right the wrongs, and to create justice for the Creator.

It is most important for you to know that you have the wonderful ability to rejuvenate and heal yourselves and others. You need not be an intellectual with academic degrees to effect cures. The formula for healing is:

Love + Harmony = Healing.

To heal others, it is essential that you have mind, body, and soul in harmony. Personal harmony allows you to take on another's pain and then let it go, without harm to yourself. Healers must train themselves to continually *absorb and release* the suffering of others. Many of you are afraid to do this, but if you do not love and care for others you will harden your own heart.

There rings within each heart and soul a special melody called the *song of soul*. It cannot be heard with the human ear. It can be heard only by the ears of your heart and soul. To heal another, listen for his song of soul and harmonize it with your own. Send this music out into the orchestra of the universe and good health will result.

Healing is simple, and I humbly ask forgiveness if I have confused you. The formula for healing comes from the Great Mathematician and is available to all of you. Your first step must be upon the pathway of understanding. Secondly, you must accept yourself and the physical and spiritual nature of your being. Healing is simple, it is a thought-form*, it is a knowingness. Thus, not only on the earth plane but in all realms, simplicity is perfection.

---

* *Thought-form* is an angelic term for a concept in your mind that is more than just a thought.

Archangel Gabriel Speaks

Second Message

Yea, it is I, Gabriel, and I come forth to speak the Word. My message today is an extension of my prior lesson on healing.

The earth and all her creatures must become as *one* with Spirit and all the universes. There are far greater universes than this one and many other forms of life. It is ludicrous for mankind to think of themselves as the only creation. As human beings depend on each other for love and respect, so also do planets. Even the stars are numbered, and if one falls from the sky it disturbs universal perfection and harmony.

It is imperative for mankind to recognize the importance of life in all its unique expressions. The earth herself is a living, breathing being, and the animals are your co-inhabitants—not merely game to be hunted. Look not with the eyes of a predator, for every living being on the planet is in danger of extinction.

From the smallest blade of grass on land to the largest

creature in the sea, each life has been predestined by the Creator. It is sad that mankind has affected the balance of nature, and even though it was done through ignorance or ego, it was done, and it must be undone. What is left to save must be cultivated and cleansed, for it will not be replaced. The restoration that took place in prior times will not occur, and the spectrum of life will be obliterated. What you term *endangered species* is yourselves.

Archangel Gabriel Speaks

Third Message

Greetings, my beloved ones. It is I, Gabriel. I come forth to speak to the leaders of this planet, and I use the term *leaders* in a liberal sense. We have only one Divine Leader.

I am here to remind you of the choices you made far before you were born. You chose to be in a position of power out of love for your fellow man. You wanted to assist the needy, deliver those unjustly imprisoned, and eliminate prejudice from society. The people have allowed you to become president, king, or queen, and you must respond with humility. For without the people you would have no power, without the Word you would have no power, and you would be powerless without the Creator.

Remember your original intentions, for soon you must deliberate on the New World Order. This order contains many words and phrases that sound attractive, but it is inconceivable for those ideas to work at this time. You are not prepared for this order to go into effect, and if it does the result will be decadence and defeat. You must consider our warning before signing the papers that will be forthcoming.

When you came to this planet your deepest desire was to serve. Your dreams were honorable, just, and righteous, but you have forgotten. Awaken your memories and the love in your heart. But if you cannot, then we from the spiritual realm ask you to step down. Hand your power to one who truly wants the best for his fellow man, his nation, and the world.

Spiritual and environmental matters are of primary importance now—not wars or defense. The virtues of truth, honesty, and unity must prevail. Lord Michael* has demanded this of you so that he may pave the way for the One who is yet to come. All countries must work together, but if one nation refuses to cooperate, then join hands with the ones that will. You must unite or the destruction that has been prophesied will take place and all about you will disappear as if it had never been. This annihilation we do not desire to do, but there is One who has control over this. We do not. We will follow the Creator. That which has been created can be destroyed, and that which the Creator has given He can take back.

Have no fear. If you are using your power in a positive direction you will have a positive outcome. I am here to reassure

---

* Michael's message was sent thirteen days before Gabriel's third message.

you of this truth. You held great love in your heart when you first began your journey here. Now you hold the key to the future. Do not forget those who are suffering, tormented, and oppressed. Do not abuse your power, and do not be deceived by promises of material gain from those who walk in darkness, for the division is at hand.

Do not look backward, only forward. Consider my words, for I speak the truth. My message will be placed before you and my words will be spoken to you. If they resonate within your heart and soul, if they awaken your memory of who you truly are in Spirit, then you will know what you must do.

Time is of the essence. The future of The Lion's Gate is up to you. We wish to keep it open so we can converse with you and continue healing your planet, for we dearly love the earth and all those upon it.

You have great challenges in the days ahead and responsibility weighs heavy on your shoulders. We ask you, with utmost sincerity, to make your decisions carefully.

Sundar Singh

ASCENDED MASTER TEACHER

An ascended master teacher is one who has passed all life's tests and returns to earth only to help others. There are many such teachers here today, and they can be recognized by their selfless devotion to others. They choose to serve, rarely asking for gratitude or appreciation, and they are too spiritually sophisticated to demand attention. They live their lives quietly performing loving deeds.

Sundar Singh specializes in teaching truth and understanding through love and compassion, and Nadira has been one of his students since she was ten years old. Sundar would appear to Nadira in visions when she was hurt or angry over a disagreement with a friend. He would comfort her and show her he understood her position. Then he would offer possible reasons for her playmate's behavior.

Sundar shed light on the situation by discussing it openly, without pity or blame. Once Nadira comprehended the dynamics involved, she was left to choose her own course of action. Sometimes hearing the facts hurt her feelings, but it gave her an awareness of human nature—her own and others. Sundar's example of kindness combined with strength, not force, enabled Nadira to empathize with her friends, and this quality has helped her in counseling clients.

Sundar's most recent lifetime was spent in Tibet. He visited Nadira shortly before his death to tell her he was going to "close my door to the earth plane." After over one hundred years as a monk, he was too tired and too cold to continue. At the time he gave the following message, he had returned to the spiritual realm.

For his speech, Sundar manifested himself in a chartreuse-colored light that continuously changed into deeper shades of gold and lighter tones of green. In the middle of these lights was a very slender blue flame. In back of Sundar were hundreds of light beings that had come together to form an arch over an altar, which was also made of light beings.

After Sundar spoke his message he addressed Nadira personally and said, "I came forth to you in your childhood years and watched you grow. Remember, all things are possible, but first you must ask."

Sundar Singh Speaks

Greetings. It is I, Sundar. I come forth in the rays of Lord Michael* to bring you truth and understanding.

Looking back on the history of earth, we see that many civilizations have come and gone. Each culture was built on words of truth, understanding, and wisdom, and each one came crashing down from words of the opposite nature. There is great power in words.

Mankind's books of knowledge do not always contain wisdom and truth, and much of what you have been taught to believe is foolish. Facts can be easily distorted, creating misunderstandings and shifting beliefs. But unless your mind, body, and soul are in harmony, you will not unlock the mysteries of wisdom, knowledge, and truth. Your eyes will be blinded from the words. Your ears will be blocked from the songs. Seek first understanding.

---

* "In the rays of Lord Michael" means that Sundar's message has been approved by Michael.

It is important for you to know that you were created to radiate light on this planet. You carry within your soul the divine light of the Creator, and it can be used by your imagination to manifest your needs and desires. Imagination is far greater than wisdom itself. Through the imagination of the Creator all things were made, and without it the earth and the universe would never have existed. Imagination is alive, it is a spirit, and it must be utilized or it will die.

In using your imagination, do not be too conservative in your dreams. Whatever you can imagine you can obtain, because there is no end to the abundance in the universe. Ask for little and you shall receive little. Ask for immense blessings and that is what you will have. But your needs must be as strong as one who is lost in the desert and thirsts after his drops of water. If you do not have this intense desire, then your dreams cannot be fulfilled.

It is essential that these messages from the spiritual realm be cherished, utilized, and circulated upon the planet. Although there will be eyes that cannot see and ears that cannot hear, there will be those who seek Spirit diligently and will use these messages to create love and peace.

I humbly ask you to accept my words.

Archangel Uriel

If you think all angels are sugar and spice and everything nice, you haven't met Uriel. Uriel is the angel in charge of the center of the earth and his job is to heal and protect his territory. In clear and certain terms, Uriel explains the disaster that awaits our planet if we do not listen to the angels.

We received two messages from Uriel, both of them hard-hitting and uncomfortable to read. They contain warnings that most of us would rather not consider, but the intention of this book is to awaken humanity to our present crisis. We were given the following message from a high angel named Zarus: "The people of earth must be shaken, and shaken hard, for they are in a deep sleep. And truly, there is no time left for them to rest."

Uriel's messages have the intensity of a panic-stricken mother who sees her child running out into the street just as a car is turning the corner. His words are strong, his tone is harsh, and he is adamant about preserving his domain. The term *tough love* could be applied to Uriel's teachings.

Nadira assumes the energy of the angel she is channeling, and for Uriel she spoke precisely and without hesitation. She raised her voice, stiffened her body, and clenched her fist. I asked afterwards why Uriel was so stern. She said, "It is very frustrating for the archangels to continuously repair the earth only to see their work undone time and again by nuclear explosions, oil spills, and the negative energy of humanity. Our love for this earth is the only thing that can save us." It is impossible to ignore the urgency of Uriel's words.

When Nadira closed her eyes to channel she saw swirling colors in brown and yellow. Brown represents the earth and signifies Uriel's planetary concerns, and yellow stands for knowledge.

Archangel Uriel Speaks

First Message

Greetings, it is I, Uriel. I come forth from the center of the earth and ask your permission to speak the Word.

(Nadira silently agrees.)

I am most thankful that you have accepted me.

Many souls have incarnated on this planet with no recollection of the ethereal realm. They have learned little on their journeys here and they are very young in spirit. But there are those who have walked this earth in many lifetimes, gathering wisdom to complete their circle of life. They are the ones I am addressing this day. Others will hear my words but will not understand them.

Earth is a living, breathing entity. It is spiritual in nature yet physical in the sense that it can be seen with human eyes, which makes it real to you. Humans must see to believe. Much of this great being has been terribly abused by mankind, beginning with its earliest inhabitants. Do not be so innocent as to think that you originated from two people. The story of Adam and Eve is a parable from the Creator, a legend for your generations.

Your recorded history is merely a blink of the eye to Spirit. There were civilizations long before Mesopotamia, and far more knowledgeable ones prior to the Valley of the Indus, but they vanished long ago. Their remains are hidden deep within the earth and will not surface for thousands of lifetimes to come, and the *karma* confronting you today is derived from those cultures.

All life in the universe falls under the Law of Cause and Effect. For every cause, be it thought, word, or deed, there is an effect. These effects, which are either positive or negative, accumulate and produce karma. Each of you is born with karma from your past lifetimes on earth, and a *karmic balance sheet* is recorded in your soul memory bank.

The earth herself contains karma, which is an electrical energy, and it must be released in a cautious manner—slowly, diligently, and in harmony with the earth's body. When karma filters out into the universe it creates a protective, electrical lining around the earth, but through technology humanity has disturbed this process and damaged the ozone layer.

Some problems have occurred, as you know, but the situation will be much worse in the future. Radiation emitting from the sun will cause great harm to the earth and its inhabitants, as it will break down the cellular structure of all living creatures. Even the mountains, oceans, and vegetation will be affected. What has happened cannot be changed, we cannot turn back the hands of time. But humanity can certainly change the future by paying homage to the earth, for if it is destroyed there will not be another.

I am here to pacify the electrical field. Archangels Michael, Raphael, Gabriel, and I are working to create the balance needed until this situation can be rectified. But when the Seals of Mystery are broken we can no longer hold our fortresses here. We will be called upon to leave. And as these seals are broken, one by one, the devastation will come and there will be afflictions upon you.

You have the technology to correct your problems. It is through greed that this knowledge has not been utilized. It is through the ignorance of those who hold the power of oil in their hands. Know they not that all will be gone? The monetary base they are seeking will disappear.

You with your greed, your oil, and your lust for power—you must now search for attainment in different avenues! Go toward the solar energies and harness them, for they will not cause disruption of the electrical field. They will not cause disease, mutations, and death.

We from the spiritual realms are working diligently to save you. Do you not want to be saved? Do you not want a future?

These are important decisions and they are facing you now. Do you not know who you are? Have you forgotten whence you came? Have your souls gone on so long that you do not remember? I will refresh your memory.

You have come from the ethereal body of the Creator to save this planet—to love one another, to overcome your negative karma, and to create the heaven this earth was intended to be. You have taken this heaven and created your own hell! And I say unto you that with the curse of time you do not have much longer. The days are numbered and only the Creator in His wisdom knows the hour. We know not, but through this channel I will tell you: It will be soon.

I am Uriel. I am the light, and I come forth with Michael—not to beseech you, not to plead with you, and not to ask you to rise above your immorality, your sinfulness, your greed, and your lust. But if you do not, the division will take place.

There will come a darkness upon this land and the ocean will rise up and die. The moon will become like blood. Pure water will be gone. Good health will not be known. You will be wretched and you will have done it to yourselves. These words I speak to you, I speak in truth. I do not wish for this tragedy to happen.

Remember who you are, where you originated, and why you are here. Overcome your material desires, cleanse this earth, and ask for the Creator's forgiveness. And remember that all of you were created in the love and perfection of the Divine One.

Archangel Uriel Speaks

Second Message

Yea, my beloved ones. I am Uriel and I come forth once more to speak to the people of this planet. I wish to plant the seeds of understanding inside your souls, and as they grow into maturity, you will harvest peace and love.

Beautiful structures have been built by mankind for prayer and spirituality, but these temples of worship have been disgraced by the jealousy and greed of members who have forbidden other people from entering. It was not intended for one denomination to feel that only they are the children of the Creator and the sun shines only on them. It is for me to inform you that all souls on this planet are smiled upon by the sun, and each one of you was brought here by the magnanimous love of the Creator.

There is not one of you who is set above or below another. You may be in high-class society, you may have great wealth, you may have political power, and you may be famous, but I say you are only privileged. When it comes time for your atonement—

the atonement comes to all people for it is part of your transition from life to death—you must atone for your feelings towards others. If you caused heartache to another through rejection and prejudice, then that is exactly what will be reflected back to you during your atonement.

It is abrasive to mankind's soul to be excluded, to be considered unacceptable, to be treated as less than a human being. And who has caused this abrasion? Who has spoken words that cut to the core of another? Who amongst you has forgotten that you are all part of the same tree? Who amongst you does not know that you all bleed, you all shed tears, and you all carry the same pain? Who amongst you can be so uncaring as to act as if you are better than another human being?

Who amongst you can smile at your fellow man, shake his hand, and welcome him to your home—then speak so rudely and with such hatred about him after he has left your lodging? Who amongst you has done this for the comfort and compliments given you from others in your circle? Who has laughed at those who are needy and poor? Many are poor only in a material sense. Their souls are rich, strong, and vigorous. Their minds are keen and intelligent. But what you do not understand you cast aside with snide remarks and hypocrisy.

You are but children and there is much for you to learn. We have boundless hope for you, but you must recognize that your behavior has been instilled in you by society. Set your standards high and do not waver from them. Establish an honorable level of integrity.

It is not your culture, your color, or your physical beauty that matters. It is not your academic achievements, how much money you give, or how many charities you fund. It is what is in your heart and soul, for the Creator knows these things, and also we in the spiritual realm.

There are many who walk in darkness and you should be careful of them. Pray for them, yes, but do not associate with them. I am speaking of those who are critical of people they do not know and fearful of ideas they do not understand. If you look for faults in another, you will always find something. Look for the best in people, not the worst. Pray for those who are bitter and angry, but do not allow your heart to become like theirs, for this is where evil plants its seeds.

There are many people who are mentally or physically handicapped, coming forth as what we term *victim souls*. They have special purposes here and you should honor them. When you see these blessed souls walking the pathways of life, do not snicker and sneer or make jest and nasty remarks. If you have the Creator within you, why can't you be kind to them? They have such love in their hearts. Take heed of my words, for in many incarnations you could have been such as they. Pray that your soul could be as pure as theirs.

When you see those who are poor and downtrodden, why

can't you help them? And must you always give to charities only when you will receive compensation? Give in the night and do not speak of it to anyone. Your offerings are between you and the Creator and not for elevation in society.

These issues have been on this planet since its beginning. There have always been those cursed with jealousy—it is the major source of evil on this planet. Jealousy is the basis of all wars. It is the basis of all murders. It is the basis of horrendous actions. The only thing close to it is fear.

I humbly ask you to listen to me with your heart and soul. Show kindness and mercy to one another, for you are all brothers and sisters.

God bless you all. I am Uriel.

Carmen

PROTECTOR OF THE ABUSED

Every bully needs a victim and, in a vicious cycle of abuse, today's victim is tomorrow's bully. The child battered by a parent or older sibling beats up on a smaller child because he has been taught that violence is acceptable. Some people have tolerated a lifetime of cruelty at the hands of others and find it very difficult to remove the yoke of oppression they have grown accustomed to wearing. Shame, fear, and depression keep many people locked in destructive, yet familiar relationships.

Many people seeking spiritual help have been abused emotionally, physically, and mentally. They look to the spiritual realm for answers, and the angels are quick to express the opinion that abuse of any nature should never be tolerated. It takes confidence and courage to stand up for ourselves and refuse ill treatment. Sometimes it is impossible for the victimized to look upon their circumstances with clarity, so Carmen's first act is to shed the light of truth on the situation. Her motto could well be, "The truth will set you free."

Once those who are abused know the truth, a feeling of self-respect begins to develop. Overcoming the confusion of lies and cover-ups that are integral in the dynamics of oppression leads victims to the next phase in the process of liberation, which is accepting responsibility for instituting change. We are all obliged to fight for our personal freedom, and Carmen and her band of angels support our efforts and are at our beck and call.

A few years ago Nadira went to the hospital to visit a client. While sitting in the waiting room she observed a young man in a cape, dancing around the room. He walked behind a group of people, spread open his cape, smiled, and sang, "Oh, how we suffer, when we think of how we suffer." Everyone was amused and happy to have the forbidding hospital atmosphere lightened with humor, but his words were true. We suffer more, not less, when we dwell on our problems.

Carmen announces her presence by appearing in a light known as *karmic blue*, which represents unresolved issues from past lifetimes. It is a bright shade of sea-blue, and it is related to emotional memories hidden deeply in the soul.

Carmen Speaks

Greetings, my beloved ones. I come forth in love to bring you enlightenment, for I am Carmen, and I have come to reveal the mystery of the Word.

Yes, my children, there are wondrous mysteries surrounding you. Many are sleeping and it is not their time to awaken, but there is one that has been quickened and it is called *suffering*. I have been given permission to disclose to you the secrets behind this word.

I come forth with the power of Lord Michael to bring comfort to the abused, to those of you suffering in mind, body, and spirit. For some of you, your spirit has been broken from extreme pain and you have lost your will to live. And some of you have been brought up believing that you will become more spiritually aware if you suffer. Please, release this thought. It is not valid or true, and it is a burden you do not have to carry. There are enough troubles on this earthly plane to contend with, please do not add more.

Your next lifetime is determined by your present existence,

and the last breath your body takes contains memories from your life on earth. Thoughts of jealousy, revenge, hatred, and agony are carried in your last breath, just as love, charity, sharing, and caring for others are also. This is all part of karma and cause and effect. Most of the children of the earth have a combination of negative and positive thought-forms. Really, this is to be expected. The Creator recognizes that you have not been placed in the best of circumstances because of the pull between light and dark—a conflict that originated at the beginning of time.

Strive to release thoughts towards others that fill you with hatred. There will always be those about you who do not value your soul and wish you harmful things. This is not to say that you should succumb to your oppressors or submit to persecution, but whether you win or lose, you will always be the victor if you do not carry anger and vengeance inside your heart. Bless those who curse and scorn you. They know not what they do, for they themselves are suffering. Pray for their souls as you pray for your own, for therein lies your peace.

It was written at the beginning of time that you blessed ones who chose to incarnate on earth should not forget this message from the ethereal realm: Love one another as you love yourself.

The Creator is the Tree of Everlasting Life and heavenly love flows like water from its branches. Drink, and you will become one with the Divine. You will put all thoughts of suffering behind you because they were created in this world by the one who hides in darkness.

Arise and awaken your soul. Create peace and harmony. And as you walk in the garden of life, plant not one seed that will come back to vex you and not bless you with a great harvest of love.

I am Carmen and I have come not only to comfort you, but to deliver you from the darkness of suffering by revealing the mystery of the Word.

Archangel Michael

Of all the celestial beings Michael is the most gentle and loving, yet the most powerful and militant. He is the Commander in Chief of the Angelic Army and he stands for truth, justice, and the heavenly way. His job is to break the darkness and illuminate the world with light, and he takes his orders directly from God. Michael loves with an intensity that is beyond human comprehension, and he is totally fearless. "Love is the answer" and "fear is an illusion" are quotations that could have originated with Michael.

Angels are completely fearless, and this is one of the traits that separates us from them. A person without fear is considered to be either a daredevil or a martyr, but angels are neither. They don't "muster up courage" so much as they simply *know* there is nothing to be afraid of. Adults tell children there is no bogeyman and everything will be all right, and angels say similar words to adults, but we're harder to convince.

We like to be frightened once in a while, otherwise we wouldn't buy tickets to see scary movies or read mystery books.

But we know that movies aren't *real* and that we can flip to the back to see how a novel ends. Angels say that nothing is real except love, and that love is all-encompassing. If we truly believed in love, we would be as wonderful as angels.

Generally Michael manifests himself as a bright, white light with a deep-blue base, but sometimes he takes on a human form. The first time Nadira saw Michael she was eighteen years old and living in a small house in Oregon. While vacuuming her avocado-green carpet she looked up to see Michael in full battle array, riding a white horse. His hair was long and blonde, his eyes crystal blue, and he was exquisitely beautiful. The house seemed to disappear before Nadira's eyes, as if by magic. Michael smiled, raised his sword, and rode off, and everything returned to normal. Nadira was filled with joy as she had prayed diligently for a visit from Michael.

Michael begins his message with his standard greeting, "I love you so." When he speaks he saturates the room, and the people in it, with his love. And always, after a visit from Michael we cry. So much love cannot be held in a human heart without spilling over.

Archangel Michael Speaks

I love you so, I love you so. The love that encompasses me I radiate upon the earth. It is a shield, it is a victory. I am that I am, for I am Lord Michael.

I come forth to enfold you in the love of my wings and to give you of my energy. When thou art lost I will deliver you. When thou art weary I will comfort you. And when your tiredness overcomes you I will pick you up, I will carry you. I am with you always, from the beginning even unto the end. I was with you in the ethereal realm and I will be with you forever.

When thou art in human form I am with you, for you breathe my being. I say to you, I say to all of you—there is not one hair on your head that is not numbered, not one hair falls that is not noted. There is not one thing of this earth—be it human, animal, plant, or mineral—that is not known by the Creator.

There is life in all things. It is a life quite different from yours, but there is life in the rocks and the trees. Everything in the universe contains life. It is only you who cannot see, but we from the heavenly levels see and feel and know all things.

Now I must speak my message for your time is growing short. I have already picked up my sword of righteousness. I have my sword in my right hand, my shield in my left. I am astride a great horse. I am prepared and you must make your preparations. There are four horsemen coming—it has been prophesied, it is the Word. These horsemen carry the Seal of Chaos that, once broken and its powers unleashed, there is no restraining. It is the opened door that cannot be closed. We have come to earth to prevent the breaking of the seal and the start of another spiritual war.

If you do not want war you must listen to us. Before taking another step forward ask yourself who you are and why you are here. You are not here for your jobs, your fancy houses, or your shiny automobiles. They have brought you nothing, they will gain you nothing. You must stop wasting precious time in meaningless pursuits.

Do not bicker amongst yourselves over gods—you all have the same God. Do not bicker over land—this earth will never be yours! The buildings can be smitten down in an instant, the land can disappear from your sight. Do you wish for this to happen? Is this what has to be for you to believe? I say it surely will and you will fall to your knees, for the rapture is at hand.

You have your decisions, my children. I do not speak to frighten you, I speak to warn you. Do you care? Your caring and love give us the strength we must have to fight for you. Go forth into the night—speak my words from the rooftops—let all mankind know. I do not speak to one of you, I speak to all of you. I love you so. Listen to me. I love you so. I am that I am, for I am Michael. I am here to defend you. I am here for the One who comes to deliver you. Blessed is the name of our God, blessed, blessed, oh so blessed. Come to me. I am waiting for you. If you are in darkness I will sanctify you. Come to me now.

*I*SAAC

SON OF SARAH AND ABRAHAM

In accordance with the divine promise, Sarah gave birth to a son when she was ninety years old and her husband Abraham was in his hundredth year of life. They named him Isaac, and he was Abraham's favorite child. When Isaac was a young boy, God commanded Abraham to take his beloved son to Moriah and sacrifice the child as if he were a lamb—in a burnt offering.

Isaac surrendered his will to his father and allowed Abraham to bind his body to a pile of wood for burning. Even though Isaac was very young, he must have known he was to take the place of the sacrificial lamb. He had seen such offerings before and still he submitted. Isaac's confidence in his father and his willingness to relinquish his life foreshadowed the crucifixion of Jesus Christ on Mount Calvary. And like Jesus, Isaac accepted his fate. As Abraham lifted the knife to slay his son, an angel appeared and stopped the execution.

Isaac's message affected us emotionally more than the others. There was such sadness and resignation in Isaac's energy, and the feeling of grief that accompanied his presence was overwhelming. Isaac's angelic assignment is to offer comfort to those who have lost loved ones through death, and he exudes tenderness and sympathy.

In attendance with Isaac were Archangel Raphael and Matthias, the apostle chosen to take the place of Judas Iscariot and now one of Gabriel's messengers. These three angels formed a triad and connected their energies to produce a clearer understanding of the following message.

When Nadira closed her eyes to begin the channeling session, she saw a long tunnel filled with various shades of green, the color for healing. Inside the tunnel was an arrow pointing straight ahead to a heart, and at the end were purple and pink lights representing spiritual love.

ing *in your heart* that those blessed souls are with the Creator, the embodiment of the I AM.

Those beloved angels gave willingly of their lives to save others upon this planet. It is sad to say, but the longer they suffered the more souls were saved, and they themselves chose how long or how many. Even though we of the angelic realm know the mysteries of life, death, resurrection, and reincarnation, still we mourn, the same as you. It causes us pain when we see you suffer, but we understand why this must be and we accept it.

There will come a day when sacrifice will not be necessary any longer. It will be when all people are united in creating a better world. I pray this day is coming soon. Mankind must come together to end this needless suffering. Please unite in your efforts to stop the deadly diseases that are rampant upon the earth, for they are becoming much worse.

I sanctify and bless these words, and I pray they will reach every ear on this earth, every heart that has ever cried out, and every soul whose song remains unsung. We shine down love upon you and ask that you surrender to the Creator.

Blessed be you that listen.

MARY
MOTHER OF JESUS

Mary, the Queen of Angels and Mother of Humanity, has left her spiritual realm many times to speak to her children on earth, and always her message is the same: Pray for peace, and love one another.

In the fifteenth century, Mary asked Dominic of Prussia to teach the world to pray holding beads she called a *Rosary*. On eighteen occasions in 1858, Mary appeared to Bernadette, a fourteen-year-old peasant girl who lived near Lourdes, France. When Bernadette asked Mary for a sign to prove to the world that she had visited her, Mary instructed Bernadette to scratch the ground. When she did, a spring of water with miraculous curative properties gushed forth.

Since then, Mary has made numerous visitations all over the world to witnesses of every color and creed. Despite her history of earthly manifestations, we were astounded when she spoke to us. Mary is of the seventh and highest heavenly level, and her lights were so dazzling Nadira had to shield her eyes. I asked Nadira to describe her journey to the Blessed Mother.

"I had to go through many gates and levels of purification before I was permitted to see Mary. First, I was led through a tunnel by a white light being in a vertical form. I followed it to a rectangular, pale blue light that encompassed my ethereal body. As I stood on this light I was transported to the green rectangle of Cosmic Consciousness, which consists of a combination of light beings and living, spiritual energies. I could see heaven, earth, and a multitude of galaxies.

"Next, I was taken through the I AM consciousness. When Spirit guides you into these lights they force you to the other side, because if you had a choice you would never leave. The I AM is profound peace and contentment, and you are made to feel like a baby wrapped up in a blanket of love. There is a sense of *knowingness*, as if all the mysteries of life are revealed to you in a single moment. The I AM consciousness cleanses you of any negativity so that you can clearly channel the thoughts of Spirit.

"Then I passed through other gates until I saw Chadeau, Matthias, and Raphael escorting Mary. Mary manifested in white, blue, and violet lights. I would like to tell you more, but her beauty is indescribable."

Mary Speaks

I am Mary and I humbly ask you to listen to my message. I wish to speak to all those blessed souls who desire enlightenment. There will be many who will raise only a deaf ear, but for those who are willing to hear words of wisdom, I will speak.

I am the Mother of Mercy and I come forth with my sorrows. I once dwelt upon the earth plane and I was very much like you. I delighted in earthly joys and pleasures, but I also felt the pain that many of you have felt or are feeling at this time. I have come to give you hope, and to assure you that there is purpose and meaning in Creation. You are wonderfully blessed, for God lives within your being. When He breathed His life into you, you became one with Him.

There have been many sorrows upon this earth. Blood has been shed by your loved ones—needlessly, and in the name of God—which is an abomination to the Creator. All violence must come to an end. Please do not fuel the fires of war any longer. Pray for your fellow man, not for your country. Cleanse your mind of all impure thoughts and pray with gladness. Send your prayers around the world so that they may connect with ours to advance peace on this planet. Together we will create a healing shield of love and protection.

The prophecies of devastation will surely come into fruition if thoughts of peace and love are not conveyed throughout the universe. Prophecies are spoken to make you aware of what could happen, and to allow you time to prevent disasters. Tomorrow can be beautiful, for the future is your canvas and you are the artist. Paint love and happiness on your portrait of life.

No one, not even the Creator, can demand that you obey our pleas because you have free will. Each of you must choose to *unite as one* with your brothers and sisters. Does this sound like a miracle? It is quite simple. In your hearts, you are all identical. There is not one amongst you who does not feel the same needs and desires. Lack of communication, hostile feelings, and worldly distractions have kept you from seeking *oneness* with the Creator and your fellow man.

Allow the goodness and love within your heart to come to the surface. Simply because there are injustices in this world does not mean that you are helpless, for you are not. You only think that you are. Do not concern yourself with the devil and his sinful ways, for he will only destroy you and all that you cherish. Chaos and destruction are the nature of the one who lies. He cannot help himself, but he can be defeated. You have dominion over evil.

It is not an enormous sacrifice for you to give me one small prayer each day. I will wrap your prayer in my wings of love and send it back to you, and I will bless you with my power to rejuvenate and heal.

Many angels have come to earth bearing gifts from the spiritual realm. Accept what they have to offer, for you will benefit greatly. It is time now that we co-create a world filled with love, harmony, and peace. Walk upon the *pathway of truth*, and do not look at the road that leads to your destruction.

Prophet Muhammad

The Archangel Gabriel appeared before Muhammad holding a tablet covered with spiritual symbols and commanded, "Read!"

"I cannot read," he replied.

Once again the heavenly messenger exclaimed, "Read!" Spirit entered Muhammad, blessed him with enlightenment, and he began to read. Gabriel delivered a series of messages on law, religion, culture, and politics, and from these teachings Muhammad composed the Koran, the sacred text of Islam. Muhammad was designated "the illiterate prophet," and he humbly accepted this appellation. While he lacked a formal education, his native intelligence and retentive memory enabled him to converse with, and influence, the most cultured members of society.

Muhammad was born in Mecca in what is now Saudi Arabia, in the year 570 and died in 632. As he lay dying he repeatedly requested, "Gabriel, come close unto me." We can only assume Gabriel answered this plea and personally escorted Muhammad to heaven. Muhammad insisted that prophets must be buried in whatever spot they died. Therefore, a grave was excavated beneath his death bed, under the room of his beloved wife Ayesha in the city of Medina.

While Muhammad was a great religious leader, he was also a war hero. He was forced into battle, even though his mission was to enlighten people through peace and love. Muhammad introduced the greeting "*Assalamu aleikum*," which translates to, "May the peace of Allah be upon you." This salutation is now spoken throughout the world.

In the following speech, Muhammad uses phrases that have been attributed to John F. Kennedy and Franklin D. Roosevelt. When we remarked on the familiarity of his words, Muhammad assured us that he was the originator of these ideas. Perhaps our two former presidents had a direct link to the spiritual realm.

Nadira was carried on an escalator constructed of light beings for her meeting with Muhammad. He was seated on a throne of white lights, and when he saw her he stood up, greeted her, then began to pace. Throughout his speech he walked back and forth, like an instructor in front of a classroom. Without a doubt, Muhammad was the most energetic Keeper of The Lion's Gate. His presence was imposing and majestic, and he radiated a gold-white light that was eight feet tall.

Chadeau chaperoned Nadira as she exited the prophet's realm, but before she left, Muhammad placed a crystal tear drop of energy inside her head. Muhammad had given Nadira a portion of his vitality, enthusiasm, and joy of life, and for almost two weeks she was inexhaustible.

Prophet Muhammad Speaks

Assalamu aleikum, my beloved one. It is I, Muhammad, and I am most honored by your presence. I have been waiting for you.

My message is from Spirit and it is universal. I will not speak of boundaries and segregation, nor of discrimination and prejudice. I will not speak of the fears and jealousies of mankind, for all these things are known to you. I will speak of greater things.

I was once in bodily form like you, and I incarnated many times upon the earth. But a lifetime on earth is of short duration because of physical impairments created through the aging process. People are under the illusion they will live forever, so they conduct themselves as if they are here for an eternity. But your days pass in a twinkling, and while you are here your works are extremely important—both to you and to the Creator. Please do not waste the precious commodity of time in obtaining money and not in acquiring spiritual growth.

I do not come forth when all is well upon the earth. Rather,

I come when there is great negativity, such as now, and this is exactly the truth of the matter. You are on the threshold of the future, and it is imperative that you step through this doorway without fear, hatred, and jealousy. Focus on the Creator and your purpose for being here. And set aside your materialistic desires, for they belittle you, discredit you, and bring you to the mercy of evil.

I have not forgotten my days here, for I made many mistakes. I pranced about with pride and vanity, for I was filled with self-importance. I saw myself as God-like, and this was my condemnation, for in lifetimes after I had to release the karma of my pompousness. Indeed, I placed myself above all that I held dear. It is easy to set aside love and Spirit, but earthly goods must be grasped quickly, lest you lose them.

It is human nature to think that Spirit will always be there and you can call on it at a later date, but let me assure you that I was just like you. I had to redeem myself and atone for my actions. I spent many lifetimes on earth until, at last, I learned humility, and that was my greatest accomplishment of all. For I did indeed learn and I did indeed humble myself to the Creator, and I did indeed follow, very diligently, the pathway that was set before me.

I taught the people about the ways of Spirit. In this book are great teachings that must be heard by those on earth, but they are not intended to become a religion, for through religion there has been much dissension. We come forth for unity, not war, and we wish for peace and love to serve the planet. Our messages come forth in simplicity and truth, and they are allowed to be given only in certain time frames. You have been given a great opportunity, and I pray that you will heed my words.

For those of you who have peeled away the layers of karma, you will be enlightened. You will hear these words and know that I am speaking truth. It is for you blessed souls to teach those who are in darkness, and to give them the hope and clarity they are seeking. There is much more to learn, this is only the beginning. You have just now entered our realm. Some of our messages may seem confusing, but they all carry noble thoughts from Spirit. All that is and all that will ever be has been created through the thoughts of the Creator, the imagination, and the I AM.

We are all here, patiently waiting, listening for a call for peace from the people on earth. We long to hear the cry for unity. If you speak it, we will come. We will surround you with our light and love, and we will shower blessings upon the planet, as we are prepared and ready to do so.

Peace has always been my mission, for I am Muhammad. I have tried diligently, through the teachings of the Creator, to represent peace upon this planet. It is time now for others to take up the books of Spirit and learn from them. Place yourself in the hands of the Creator and ask what you can do to serve mankind, not what mankind can do for you. Rather, ask what you can do to serve mankind, the Creator, and the universe. Do not worship us, I beseech you. It is not for you to bow down before us. Rather, we bow down before you, for we look upon each of you and see the Creator's light in your souls. We are here to help you, and we are here to remind you why you are here.

Salaam.

VYADA

UNIVERSAL MASTER TEACHER

Angels exist in a world without time—past, present, and future are one in their reality. This is a difficult concept to understand, but it can be illustrated in physical terms. Imagine a boat floating down a river that has many bends and curves. People on the boat cannot see around the next bend and the obstacles that lie ahead of them. The stretch of river behind the curve they have just passed is also out of their sight. Only a short distance in front of them is within their view.

Flying overhead is a plane and the passengers on board can look down on the entire river scene. They see where the boat has been, where it is going, and its present position. To them, everything is happening at once and their perspective is different from those on the boat.

Vyada is a long-distance space traveler. Her home is in a realm very far away, but still part of the celestial domain. She is an emissary from Melchizedek, who is a powerful, creative force in the universe. In the very near future, earth will enjoy the special qualities that are bestowed by Melchizedek's energy. We will graduate from a three-dimensional reality and progress into the fourth, which offers superior love, peace, and understanding.

Vyada made several attempts to speak to Nadira, but her frequency was too high for a clear transmission. When Vyada finally made contact, she came through with an enormous burst of energy and startled Nadira. It was as if a sudden electrical storm had struck. Vyada adjusted her frequency and Nadira successfully translated for her.

Vyada appeared in a rosy-red hue, and when she extended her wings, her colors changed to purple. Her essence is feminine but she possesses a great deal of masculinity. She serves as a reminder that we all have both male and female energies, and both are equally valuable.

Vyada Speaks

Behold, it is I, Vyada. I come forth to you from the realm of Melchizedek to speak the Word.

Life cannot exist without love, and the source of all love is the Creator, the embodiment of the great I AM. In the beginning this planet was in total darkness, and the Creator and His workers brought forth light and love. The light blended with the darkness to provide a harmonious balance for the creation of life.

At this time the darkness again outweighs the light, and instead of a perfect blending there is a divide. It is important that this division not grow any wider. The division of good and evil, which has been prophesied, will cause cataclysmic changes on earth. It is not too late to change the course of destiny, and we are here to help you. By uniting together in love and peace you can balance the scales.

"How can we do this?" you ask. Begin within your own realm by showing your family love, charity, and patience. Be of strong moral character and your loved ones will indeed follow in your footsteps. Your neighbors will be influenced by your family's example and peace will grow and flourish. Some say that co-dependency is wrong, but there is not one amongst you who is completely independent. Each one of you relies upon another, do you not?

Be loyal and true to your homeland. Those of you living in the country of your interpreter are quite blessed, as your founders were spiritually enlightened. Each one received a message from Spirit, and together they wrote the Constitution on parchment. Carry these laws close to your heart. Protect your rights to life, liberty, and the pursuit of happiness. These are key words and they are coming under attack at this time. If you do not pay attention, there will come a great fire, and you will see the words on the papers burn as if you had set your own torch to them. Their ashes will be carried away with the wind.

The Creator came forth upon this planet to evolve a beautiful garden, and He gave the inhabitants free will. He asked only for their obedience to His laws. Mankind disobeyed by choosing knowledge over everlasting life, and this unfortunate choice brought them death. This is neither here nor there in the destiny of the world, but it did circumscribe a time frame. Before this event there was timelessness.

Each man and woman born upon this planet is given an allotment of time prior to their birth. Even though you incarnate lifetime after lifetime, so many of the early years are used relearning the fundamentals of existence that there is very little time left to perform your spiritual works.

Before your birth, while you are still on the ethereal realm, you choose a *life intention*, an attribute you want to obtain in this particular lifetime. Then the *veil of forgetfulness*, which is necessary for you to concentrate on acquiring your chosen attribute, is placed over you and you begin your journey to earth. Consciously you cannot remember your life intention, but on a subconscious level you know you have work to do during your years on this earth.

So you go about performing your task, not fully knowing what you are supposed to accomplish or how many days you have to complete your assignment. This is confusing and frustrating for you, we ask for your patience. We have come to help you remember why you are here, but we cannot impose our will upon you. You must be quiet and still and listen for our voices.

Each of you must look within to find your heart and soul's *true desire*. This knowledge will bring you inner peace. Before you make your transformation back to the ethereal realm, you must try to make this world a better place for all. Do not waste your precious time with the trivialities and distractions of everyday living. Those things are not of importance to Spirit.

We have come forth from the spiritual realm to assure you that there is life after death. I promise you this, for I am Vyada. We are so thankful to each precious one of you for your courage in being on the earth plane at this time of transition. We glorify you and ask that you accept your own brilliance. Make happiness your cloak and wear it shining bright for all the universe to see. Let honor rule your mind. Let love rule your heart. Allow the Creator to reward you with His blessings.

It is such a joy to watch your awakening. We rain down blessings upon you, we love you. Let our love envelop you and carry you forward into a new garden of life.

Selah.

Queen Esther

On the seventh day of feasting, when King Ahasuerus of ancient Persia was merry with wine, he commanded that Queen Vashti be adorned with the crown jewels and brought before his court. Vashti refused, which infuriated the king and led to the loss of her royal title. Commissioners were appointed to bring all the beautiful young virgins to the citadel of Susa where the king would choose his new wife.

Esther, an exquisitely lovely girl and the adopted daughter of a Jew named Mordecai, won the admiration of all who saw her, including the king. She was chosen over the others to be queen of a kingdom that stretched from India to Ethiopia.

Shortly after this event, Haman of Agag, a high-ranking official in the palace, was greatly angered by Mordecai's failure to pay him homage. In his fury he sought to destroy all the Jews for the disobedience of one. He persuaded King Ahasuerus to issue a decree ordering the killing of every man, woman, and child of the Jewish race.

Upon hearing this news Esther was overcome with grief.

Mordecai sent her a message asking her to implore the king's favor and plead with him for her people. Esther was afraid to approach the king in the inner court without being summoned because the penalty was death, but Mordecai insisted that she do as he asked. When Esther entered the court and saw the displeasure of Ahasuerus, she fainted. The king was overcome with compassion and said to Esther, "Tell me what you desire. Even if it is half my kingdom, it is yours for the asking."

"If it pleases your majesty, grant me my life and the lives of my people."

The Jews were saved, Mordecai was placed second in charge to the king, and Haman and his ten sons were hanged. Esther, a young woman in the year 473 B.C., was credited with delivering the Jewish nation from extinction.

Today Queen Esther sits on a throne made of lights and vibrantly colored jewels and gemstones. When she met with Nadira she was arrayed in a splendor of purple—the color of royalty. Esther is very generous with her ethereal possessions. She placed a pearl of knowledge on Nadira's crown, gave her a red stone, and said, "Take this ruby and swallow it. Your tongue will speak only words of love, wisdom, and enlightenment."

Queen Esther Speaks

Behold, it is I, Esther. I have come forth for you and your book, as I too have a message. It may seem controversial but it is a message that needs to be spoken.

It is written in your Holy Books that in the beginning mankind was given dominion over all the earth and its creatures. This was a gift bestowed upon the people by the Creator. As you know from the parable of Adam and Eve, mankind chose to eat of the Tree of Knowledge and not the Tree of Everlasting Life, thereby constituting the *curse of time* and forfeiting their power of dominion to Lucifer.

Lucifer was held in high esteem by the Creator and was like the Creator Himself. During the great Heavenly War, Lucifer came upon this earth and placed it in darkness. The Creator had to come forth and radiate light to counterbalance the darkness and save the planet. He created beings of light on the heavenly planes and gave them life, and they assumed bodies and came to this garden called earth to equalize the evil. But rather than obeying the Creator or even listening to what He was saying, they carelessly handed over their power to Lucifer.

All this was in the beginning. Now we are approaching another spiritual war between Lucifer and the Creator. Those of you on the planet who are *light workers* are extremely angry about this chain of events. Stirring inside you is a rage derived from the distress of being placed upon this planet in its present condition, and the injustice of being expected to right the wrongs of those who disobeyed God.

You have our compassion, truly. We understand your fears and confusion, but you have no time to dwell on the past. You must prepare for what is yet to come. You must fight—with all you have within you—to regain your power of dominion, to fight for your very souls, and to fight for the Creator. I am not speaking of defending your country but of combating evil. Evil is rampant in all societies in every nation around the world.

Many of you question the Creator. "How could an all-powerful, benevolent being allow such things as wars, disease, and tragedies?" And even, "Why should His children endure heartaches, unhappiness in their homes, and frustration in their jobs?" If you are waiting for divine intervention you will be sadly disappointed. You were given the ability to fend for yourselves and it was given to you divinely.

In the past you gave away your power of dominion to Lucifer. How many times do you expect to be given this authority only to cast it aside? You are living in the aftermath of decisions made so carelessly so very long ago. Your bitterness should be directed at those who caused your problems. They thought they were smart, they thought they were clever, but they were very foolish.

"How could they have been so ignorant?" you ask. "How could they have been so deceived?" Well look around you, for there is deceit everywhere. There is deception is all aspects of your media. You cannot believe what you read or see or hear, for many times you have been given information that has proved to be false.

We of the angelic realm have come forth to speak the truth. Every word in this book is true. There will be those of you who will laugh and scorn. We will pray for you. But there will be others who will read our messages with their hearts and souls, and their lives will be changed.

If there were anything on heaven or earth we could do for you, we would do it. We would do it gladly, but these are your works. You have incarnated upon this earth plane to overcome the deeds of your ancestors for your own benefit and the sake of your children.

I know exactly how you feel. I lived on this earth. I bore children, I fought wars, and I stood up for the rights of my people, for I am Queen Esther. I suffered greatly, but so much is learned from heartbreak.

Do not put your faith in anyone but God, for only love and

all that is good comes from Him. How can humanity accuse the Creator of imposing such pain and sorrow on a planet He created in love? Remember, you have done this to yourselves. Take back your dominion!

REFLECTIONS

Ask and you shall receive

When the angels informed me that I was their "scribe," I told them they had made a mistake: "I don't know how to write, I have too many personal problems to concentrate on, and I have to find a job." Feeling good about my excellent reasons for declining their invitation and certain that the matter was settled, I tried to move on with my life, but I couldn't make any progress. Everything I attempted to do seemed to be blocked by insurmountable obstacles. And a voice inside my head kept nagging, "You can learn to write, you shouldn't dwell on your troubles, you have nothing better to do than talk to angels."

I finally conceded. "OK, angels. I'll work for you, but you have to make it easy on me."

Whether it was divine providence or a series of coincidences I don't know, but I decided to leave the suburbs and move into a condominium in downtown Portland, Oregon. In my building lived a bestselling author who became my closest friend, the central library temporarily relocated next door, and various newspapers (none of which I subscribed to) mysteriously appeared on my doorstep containing pertinent articles about angels.

Seek and you shall find

"Each one of you on the earth plane has chosen your own unique pathway to Spirit. You are all different, and there is a perfect path for each of you. It was of your own choosing," reported my guardian angel Dalia, "to follow all sorts of avenues and all methods of teaching."

With the library easily accessible, I began researching angels. "It takes half a library to write one book," my writer friend told me. There is so much to learn about any given subject, and the number of books, magazine articles, songs, plays, and movies written about angels is truly amazing. I specifically sought out information about personal experiences with the celestial realm, and I found a single common thread—simplicity. Sometimes there was a lot of fanfare preceding an angelic proclamation and sometimes not, but angels themselves always spoke directly, using simple terms that were easy to understand.

Maybe angels know that if they give us too many words to play with we will convolute their messages. Our minds have become so confused by the lies we have been told—whether they are little white lies or enormous distortions of the facts—that we have lost trust. And nothing is more damaging to a relationship than a lack of faith.

Knock and it shall be opened to you

My days of writing for the angels passed by quickly and smoothly. Nadira, after completing the channeling process in the first eighty-three days, contributed to other sections of the book. My writer friend offered advice on grammar and paragraphing, and my sister Patty Wolfe found the perfect illustration for the introduction to the *Keepers*. Even the art represented another coincidence. Over twenty years ago an artist named Gary Wolfe (no relation to Patty and me) painted a picture of a lion behind a wrought-iron gate and titled it *The Lion's Gate*. Patty bought the painting and graciously allowed us to modify it to fit this book.

My concerns about the book were beginning to dissipate, but there was one small item we had failed to seriously consider—publishing. At the time of this writing, that question has yet to be answered. But you are holding this book in your hands, so you know how our story ends. There is only one thing left to say.

Ask for help. Angels will answer you.

Seek the spiritual path. Angels will light your way.

Knock on heaven's door. Angels will open a world of love and peace that was created for you.

THE AUTHORS

Nadira Duran

Nadira was born into a materially poor, but spiritually enlightened family in a small town in California. Both her mother and her grandmother were born with a caul, the symbol of second sight. For eleven days after Nadira's birth, her body glowed and people called her the "baby with magic skin." At the age of three, Nadira told Bible stories and spoke prophecies from the pulpit in her church. Nadira received the gift of channeling in 1986, and since then has interpreted over two thousand messages from angels.

Nadira is the mother of six children and lives in Oregon where she works as a teacher, a healer, and a messenger for the angels.

Donna Wolfe

Donna was born in Pennsylvania to traditional Catholic parents. Her love of the Christian faith overflowed into a curiosity about religion and the nature of spirituality. After a profound near-death experience, Donna began a spiritual search that culminated in Oregon where she found Nadira. During a personal channeling, Donna's guardian angel Dalia announced that the angels were going to send universal messages for a book, and Donna was the chosen scribe.

Donna is the mother of four grown children and lives in Oregon.